Original title:
The Compass of Timeless Truth

Copyright © 2025 Creative Arts Management OÜ
All rights reserved.

Author: Alec Davenport
ISBN HARDBACK: 978-3-69081-084-5
ISBN PAPERBACK: 978-3-69081-580-2

Time's Embrace on the Soul's Journey

In a world where clocks just spin and spin,
I lost my map on a whim, not a sin.
I chased a second, thought it was the best,
But it turned out to be just a darned jest.

I asked a turtle for directions quite nice,
He chuckled and said, 'Just roll the dice!'
With each tick-tock, a giggle ensued,
Time's sense of humor is wildly pursued.

Through past and future, I wandered about,
But the present was shy, and filled with a pout.
It told me, 'Why fret over lost moments, dear?
Just eat some ice cream, and I'll reappear!'

When clocks go backwards, that's truly a laugh,
I saw my younger self doing the math.
We danced in the rhythm of time's silly game,
And high-fived my wrinkles, embracing the fame!

Navigating Shadows of Wisdom

In the fog of thought, we roam,
Lost in riddles, far from home.
A squirrel speaks, a tree gives advise,
Wit wrapped in bark, oh what a surprise!

Tickle the stars with a pun so grand,
Dance in the moonlight, join the band.
Knowledge hides in a joker's jest,
Laughter is wisdom's secret quest!

Paths Woven Through Time

On roads where clocks laugh and play,
Time trips us up in a zany ballet.
With shoes made of jelly and socks of cheese,
We waddle along, quite eager to please.

Each step is a giggle, each stumble a cheer,
Winding through moments, we hold dear.
Past and present do the cha-cha slide,
In this wacky route, we surely take pride!

Celestial Guides of the Heart

Stars wear hats, and comets do cheer,
A galaxy whispers, 'Come dance over here!'
With martians on scooters, what a delight,
They say, 'Join our party, we groove all night!'

Planets play tag, on a cloud made of cream,
While the sun makes toast, it's quite the dream.
Galactic giggles buzz through the air,
Every heartbeat beats without a care!

Beyond the Horizons of Illusion

Where rabbits wear glasses, and wise owls fly,
We sail on a breeze, with no reason why.
Past laughter and nonsense, wherever we roam,
Every mental hiccup feels just like home.

The horizon winks, with a cheeky grin,
Saying, 'Dive in buddy, let the games begin!'
Illusions dance, in a whimsical spree,
Where each twist and turn is the best way to be!

Timeless Voyagers

In a boat made of cheese, we set sail,
With a captain who thinks he's a whale.
Our map is a doodle, all scribbled and torn,
But laughter's the wind that keeps us reborn.

With each wave that splashes, we giggle and cheer,
Finding treasures of giggles, scattered like deer.
The stars in the sky are just dots of delight,
While jellyfish dance in the soft, moonlit night.

The Whispering Winds of Insight.

The breeze brings us secrets from ages ago,
Like socks that went missing, they wander too slow.
We chase after wisdom like it's a lost kite,
But it flips and it flops, oh what a sight!

Squirrels join in, wearing hats made of nuts,
While owls give advice, though they're also just struts.
Each gust holds a story, most oddly spun,
In a realm where the serious forget how to run.

North Stars and Inner Journeys

Navigating dreams where the bananas can chat,
We ponder our purpose while patting a cat.
The map is a mirror that shows us our frown,
As the compass points inward, we're turned upside down.

With each twist and turn, we laugh at our fate,
Chasing shadows of popcorn that lead us to gates.
With giggles as guides and silliness supreme,
Our travels through time feel like a silly dream.

Echoes of Eternal Light

In a realm where the echoes wear shoes made of sound,
We dance with our shadows, all jumbled around.
Each giggle's a beacon, guiding us on,
As we whirl through the ages from dusk until dawn.

With clocks made of jelly and sunshine for clocks,
We chase after rabbits in bright, polka-dots.
The echoes ring out, 'Don't take life too tight!'
In this world of pure nonsense, everything's bright!

Alchemy of the Infinite Self

In a pot of soup, add dreams and glee,
Stirring laughter, oh so carefree.
Mix in the quirks, the curious blend,
What's in your kitchen? Just ask a friend.

A dash of silliness, a pinch of flair,
While whisking time without a care.
Brewing mischief in the sunset's glow,
The secret potion? Go with the flow!

Embraces of the Past and Future

Yesterday danced in a polka suit,
While tomorrow wore funky combat boots.
Together they giggled, a mischievous sight,
In a timeless waltz, day turned to night.

With shadows from ages, they twirled about,
Confused the cat, left the dog in doubt.
"Time's a prankster!" the duo declared,
As they pulled on the strings of what was and shared.

Signposts of the Ancient Light

A signpost stood in a field of cheese,
Pointing to nowhere, oh what a tease!
"Turn right for giggles, left for a snack,"
The ancient light shimmered, "Don't look back!"

With arrows of laughter to guide their way,
Through ticklish sunlight of yesterday's play.
The map was a riddler, a whimsical jest,
Who knew getting lost was a treasure quest!

Memoirs of the Ever-Flowing Stream

Once a stream wore a jester's hat,
With ripples of giggles, quick and sprat.
Drifting along with a cheerful shout,
"Why be serious? It's fun to pout!"

Pages of water, stories of cheer,
Flowing in circles, Oh dear! Oh dear!
Casting reflections of silly old days,
As frogs croaked sonnets in muddy displays!

Rhythms of the Unending

In a land where clocks all giggle,
Time dances like a silly wiggle.
Each hour wears a vibrant hat,
While minutes chase a playful cat.

Seconds jump like frogs in rain,
Singing songs that are quite insane.
A tick-tock here and tock-tick there,
Laughter floats upon the air.

Every tick is full of cheer,
As time itself just disappears.
With no worries, we just play,
Who cares what day is judgment day?

So let the silly rhythms flow,
Through fields of joy, we laugh and grow.
In this world where jokes are ripe,
We shape our fate with jokes and hype.

Dreams of an Ageless Land

In a world where no one ages,
The trees read books in worn-out pages.
The clouds wear glasses, wise and clear,
While flowers whisper, "No need to fear!"

The sun just smiles, it won't grow tired,
In dreams of youth, we are inspired.
The rabbits dance, their shoes are tight,
While birds recite poetry at night.

Time there wears a jester's cap,
We nap beneath the old time map.
The mountains giggle, oh what a sound,
In this land, joy is always found.

So close your eyes and dream away,
In ageless lands where we all play.
With chuckles ringing in the skies,
Life is one big, bright surprise.

Lightkeepers of Forgotten Truth

We forge our path with shining giggles,
Keeping secrets where the time wiggles.
With lanterns made of laughter bright,
We chase the shadows into the light.

Each truth we find is wrapped in wraps,
Like bouncing balls that yield strange flaps.
Old tales told by a wobbly sage,
Turn serious facts into a fun stage.

In corners where the past sits still,
We tickle time with every thrill.
So come along, and never pout,
We'll shine the truth, of that no doubt!

With every blink of starry skies,
We find the truth wrapped in goodbyes.
A giggle here, a chuckle there,
The lightkeepers dance without a care.

Journeys Beyond the Veil

Oh, what a ride beyond the veil,
With silly ghosts that tell a tale.
They flap their sheets, and dance about,
Saying, "Join us, there's no doubt!"

We skip on clouds of fluffy whim,
Where laughter sparkles, bright and dim.
The wind blows jokes that never cease,
As we roam in quest for peace.

Through portals where the odd things meet,
We find the truth beneath our feet.
A ticket stamped with giggles loud,
Shows journeys made with a silly crowd.

So hold on tight, don't lag behind,
In veils of laughter, truth you'll find.
Each step a dance, each turn a jest,
In journeys beyond, we are the best!

Fables of the Ever-Present

In a land where clocks all dance,
Squirrels ponder, 'Was that a chance?'
Dogs wear glasses, claim they see,
The future's bright, or is it me?

Cats in suits debate profound,
While turtles race, but don't leave ground.
Each moment waits, a silly tease,
To make us laugh, oh mighty breeze.

Fish wear hats and juggle flies,
While goats give speeches, oh my, oh my!
We giggle as the seconds sway,
In a world where time just wants to play.

So gather 'round, let tales be spun,
Of timeless truth in jokes and fun.
With laughter echoing through the loam,
We find ourselves, we feel at home.

Pioneers of the Eternal Quest

A goat in boots maps out the course,
While ants discuss their mighty force.
A squirrel claims he's found the way,
To shorten naps to half a day!

The mice are all on Google Maps,
Debating snacks and epic traps.
Raccoons with charts and pie in hand,
Plotting paths through the junkyard land.

Unicorns with comical grace,
Attempt to juggle in a race.
Through timeless trees and bamboo trails,
They share their dreams of glittery gales.

So join the dance, join the jest,
In a quest that brings out our best.
With every laugh and silly cheer,
We'll find the truths that bring us near.

Lanterns of the Unfathomable Night

In the dark, a lightbulb sings,
While owls wear capes with sparkling wings.
Stars are busy playing cards,
In cosmic games that leave us charred.

Bats in bowties twirl and spin,
While moonbeams laugh and play to win.
Each shadow chuckles, throws a jest,
At those who think they know what's best.

The night is filled with wacky scenes,
As crickets host their lively means.
A glow-worm glows, not out of fright,
But to lead folks toward laughter's light.

So wander where the lanterns play,
In the whims of night, we lose our way.
With every giggle in the dark,
We unravel truths with a spark.

Portals of the Timeless Mind

In a realm where thoughts do glide,
Mindful fish just take it in stride.
Each worry fades like candy floss,
While ideas clash, and none are lost.

A parrot squawks, 'The sky's the limit!'
While dreams take flight, oh what a skit!
Thoughts tick and tock like playful clocks,
In the circus vibe, we all unbox.

Pigs with glasses ponder the past,
As laughter echoes, never fast.
Through portals wide, our minds explore,
A funny realm with room for more.

So step right up and join the fun,
In the quest for truths, we've just begun.
With every chuckle we unwind,
To find the depths of a timeless mind.

Tides of Eternity

The clock ticked loud, but who can hear?
Time's a jester, full of cheer.
It walks in circles, round and round,
And leaves us lost, but oh so found.

In jelly shoes and with green hats,
We chase the seconds like silly cats.
The sun's a friend, but it likes to hide,
While we dance on waves, a silly ride.

A turtle's race, quite slow and fun,
He tells me tales of times undone.
With laughter loud, we shed our frowns,
In seas of joy, we splash and drown.

So here's to moments, silly and bright,
For in the end, it's all pure light.
We ride the tides, with laughter's spark,
In the vast ocean, we leave our mark.

Horizons Unfolding

Oh look, a map, all tattered and torn,
With doodles of palm trees and unicorns worn.
We'll sail at dawn, or maybe at noon,
And accidentally land on the moon!

With snack packs ready and silly hats,
We'll navigate through giant bats.
Each wave whispers silly little tunes,
While crabs tap dance under the moons.

Our compass spins in circles all day,
It points to cupcakes, come what may.
Lost in giggles, each silly breeze,
We'll find treasure in peanut butter trees.

So hoist the sails, let's set the stage,
For every turn is a brand new page.
With laughs as our maps, we sail away,
In pursuit of joys that never sway.

The Uncharted Voyage

We set our sails with pizza in hand,
On an uncharted trip to Snackland.
An island made of candies, I swear,
But the parrot just sings about underwear!

With every wave, we toast our drinks,
Life's a riddle filled with winks.
The wind whispers secrets, or is that a joke?
We're lost on purpose, or was that a bloke?

Each star's a guide, with a silly grin,
They twinkle at us as we spin.
A treasure chest filled with chocolate glee,
We'll crack it open, just wait and see.

So here's to the folly, the fun, and the cheer,
In this wacky voyage, we've nothing to fear.
With laughter our anchor, we ride the tide,
For in joy and silliness, we shall abide.

Shadows of Forgotten Realms

In shadows where giggles roam,
We find our way, through realms unknown.
A dragon sneezed, and what a sight,
With sparkles and glitter, it took flight!

The ghosts in capes, they waltz and prance,
Inviting us all to join the dance.
With tickles and chuckles, they glide on by,
In this whimsical world, we soar and fly.

A castle built of marshmallow fluff,
With pudding moats, can't get enough.
Jesters juggle in the moon's bright glow,
As midnight snacks begin to flow.

So here's to shadows that sway and shimmy,
To forgotten realms where life feels zippy.
With laughter our sword, we face the night,
For in every giggle, we find the light.

The Symphony of Infinite Roads

I took a turn at every street,
A map alone can't help my feet.
With every wrong, a giggle grew,
Who knew lost paths lead to a zoo?

In search of coffee, I found a cat,
He gave directions, 'Just follow that.'
But all he meant was a nap to take,
Now I'm here, awake—what a mistake!

One bend led to a sandwich shop,
And oh, the snacks just made me stop.
A picnic dance, with ants in tow,
A party without a place to go!

So here I am, in life's wild race,
With every turn, I lose my place.
But laughter echoes in my shoes,
A joyful heart, I cannot lose!

Lyrics from the Timeless Realm

In a world where clocks seem shy,
I asked a tree, 'Oh, tell me why?'
It rustled leaves and grinned a grin,
'Who needs time? Just let the fun begin!'

I danced with shadows, played with light,
Sipped on starlight, felt so right.
Each tick-tock turned into a joke,
A laugh, a smile, no need to choke!

Old stones whispered secrets true,
But all I heard was 'Boo-hoo-hoo!'
They cracked me up with tales from yore,
Of socks that vanished, nevermore!

So here I roam, no worries here,
The past is funny, let's give a cheer.
In timeless tunes, I find my way,
With quirky rhymes that never sway!

Chronicles of the Eternal Traveler

Once I set out for lands unknown,
With pie in hand and seeds I'd sown.
Each step I took was full of cheer,
But then my shoe decided to veer!

It dance a jig, then kicked a rock,
I laughed so hard, I missed the clock.
A rabbit hopped and joined the spree,
We both agreed, 'Time's just a flea!'

Chasing whims and silly dreams,
I stumbled on a river of creams.
I swam in laughter, splashed with glee,
No need for maps, just follow me!

Onward I went with friends so bright,
In a world where silliness takes flight.
Every twist and turn, a joke to share,
Eternal follies, without a care!

Guardians of the Hidden Path

They told me secrets of the stars,
Yet all I heard were giggling Mars.
I bumped into a wise old crow,
He cackled loud, 'Just go with flow!'

The hedges hummed a catchy tune,
As shadows danced beneath the moon.
Each step revealed a silly sight,
A lost balloon, a cat in flight!

With every twist, a laugh would spring,
Like silly songs that make you sing.
The hidden path, a joke, a riddle,
All life's punchlines played so middle!

So join the fun on this wild ride,
With whimsy flowing like the tide.
Guardians of giggles lead the way,
On paths of joy, come out to play!

Beyond the Veil of Illusion

In a world where socks go wild,
A mismatched pair is quite the style.
The truth hides here and dances about,
Behind the curtain, full of doubt.

Those shiny things that glitter bright,
Like brains, they vanish in the night.
Yet in our hearts, we hold the key,
To unlock what's funny, wild, and free.

With laughter ringing round our heads,
We find our way through tangled threads.
The trick is really not to tread,
On eggshells made of stinky bread.

So here we wander, side to side,
With giggles as our trusty guide.
While searching for what's really true,
Remember, it could just be you!

The North Star of Wisdom

A dot of light up in the sky,
Looks like a bug that learned to fly.
With wisdom wrapped in silly hats,
It craves attention from the cats.

In fields where cows wear shoes of lace,
We ponder life at a brisk pace.
The stars might giggle as we sigh,
But wisdom's got a great disguise.

Slide down that rainbow, make a wish,
And sip some tea from a fishy dish.
The path is paved with candy treats,
Where knowledge dances on sticky feet.

So let's embrace this cosmic jest,
And welcome laughter as our guest.
For wisdom is a playful sprite,
Leading us through the comical night.

Labyrinths of Yesterday

In mazes filled with ancient dust,
We stumble forth in purest trust.
A map with doodles, winks, and spins,
Leads us to where the fun begins.

Old memories tangle like dark vines,
Traces of trips to pizza shrines.
The laughter echoes through the trees,
As we recall our funny misdeeds.

With every twist, a giggle grows,
From tales of friends and silly woes.
We dance around the corners tight,
Playing tag with ghosts of light.

So if you wander, don't despair,
Those labyrinths are but a dare.
Find joy in every path you take,
And let your silly laughter shake!

The Silent Guide

In silence where the squirrels play,
A wisdom lingers day by day.
Yet all they do is snack and climb,
Finding nuts is their only crime.

A gentle breeze whispers nearby,
Waking truths that want to fly.
But often truth wears socks askew,
And answers dance in a funny shoe.

With every blink, the world's a jest,
Where foolish thoughts are free to rest.
The guide is silent, but it knows,
That laughter's fragrance always grows.

So skip along with quirk and cheer,
Embrace the nonsense that draws near.
For in the quiet, truth will giggle,
As shadows play and jiggle, jiggle!

The Lighthouse of Insight

In a foggy head, where thoughts get stuck,
A lighthouse shines, oh what good luck!
It flashes bright, with humor in tow,
Navigating life's absurd flow.

With a beacon's blink, 'Hey, watch your toes!'
It warns of pitfalls, where reason goes.
Lost socks, odd snacks, all life's little quirks,
Illuminated by a guide that smirks.

Laughter erupts like waves on the shore,
It's clear we're quirky, can't ignore.
In the harbor of sanity, we dock and jive,
With insights aglow, we laugh and thrive.

So heed the light, don't get too lost,
In the curious sea of what it costs.
For wisdom can tickle, that's the plan,
At the Lighthouse of Insight, just be a fan!

Celestial Bearings

Stars twinkle like sequins in a cosmic dance,
They wink and giggle, say, 'Take a chance!'
Orbiting truths, in giggles wrapped tight,
Navigating nonsense, in the starry night.

With planets that grin, and comets that race,
They guide our ship, in this silly space.
"Pick the right one!" a star shouts in glee,
"Just don't ask me where the snacks might be!"

Constellations chuckle at each misstep,
As we stumble along, mapping with pep.
With humor as fuel, we sail through the vast,
In celestial bearings, our doubts are outclassed!

So next time you gaze at the night's silly show,
Remember the punchlines the heavens bestow.
In the cosmic chaos, have a laugh or two,
Celestial bearings will guide you true!

Discoveries Beyond Time

In a quirky lab where clocks do spin,
Time's got a giggle just waiting to win.
With seconds that dance and minutes that shake,
Every tick brings a laugh, and then a quake.

Scientists chuckle at paradoxes bold,
While drafting blueprints of stories untold.
"Wait, what year is it?" a voice will declare,
"Does it really matter? Let's just do hair!"

Every moment's a treasure, it seems absurd,
As they jumble and fumble; oh, haven't you heard?
In the attic of time, lost slippers are found,
With discoveries sparking laughter profound.

So, venture with gusto, where moments rewind,
In discoveries bold, let silly intertwine.
For in the fabric of time, pure joy stays,
Tickling the timelines in whimsical ways!

The Journey Through Veils

Through veils of confusion, laughter will lead,
On a journey so wacky, just follow the creed.
With each layer peeled, absurd truths await,
Like finding a sandwich on a lost dinner plate.

Skipping past riddles and goofy old myths,
Each step reveals joy, like unexpected gifts.
"Who thought this path would get so silly?"
Bursting with laughter, our minds are so frilly!

Peeking beyond shadows, seeing what's there,
In this playful quest, life's never a scare.
With humor our guide, we glide through the haze,
Unveiling the truth in the most fun-filled ways.

So join in the dance, don't shy away now,
Our veils of confusion will take a bow.
Through laughter and lightness, joy will unveil,
On this whimsical journey, we'll merrily sail!

Harmonies of Ages Unseen

In a world where socks disappear,
And toast lands butter-side near,
Time dances on a hula hoop,
While cats conspire with the soup.

The clock ticks backward on its own,
Telling tales we've never known,
A peacock struts in rainbow socks,
And wisdom hides inside the clocks.

Yesterdays wear mismatched shoes,
Discovering paths we never choose,
In worlds where laughter echoes wide,
With penguins wearing crowns of pride.

So let us twirl and prance like sprites,
With quirky dreams and silly sights,
For in this realm of giggles and glee,
Truth is wobbly as can be!

Plumb Lines of Existence

A ruler sits beneath a tree,
Measuring joy and baked brie,
Squirrels shout their wild debate,
While the universe checks its weight.

Frogs are wearing tiny shoes,
Charting paths they cannot choose,
Fish gossip deep in the stream,
On the nature of the dream.

Time can waltz on jellybeans,
And juggle all our playful scenes,
Each tick a giggle, each tock a dance,
As monkeys plan their next big chance.

In cosmos where the absurd blends,
With laughter that never ends,
Existence wears a silly crown,
As we jest and tumble down!

The Horizon of Unfurling Truth

Distant shores of wisdom call,
While clams learn to stand up tall,
Seagulls debate with grateful trees,
Over sandwiches and warm breezes.

Truth's a kite that flies so high,
Spinning tales in the open sky,
While turtles surf on jelly waves,
And time misbehaves like playful knaves.

Crabs dance with their claws held wide,
In quest of snacks they cannot hide,
With every sunset painting the scene,
Life's an endless giddy routine.

So let's run along the sandy shore,
Searching for laughter, always more,
For each moment glimmers anew,
Chasing the silly, the funny, the true!

Threads of the Infinite Tapestry

In a loom spun by cosmic jest,
The fabric of life holds every quest,
We stretch our yarns, oh what a sight,
With plucky jokes that take to flight!

Spiders weave in hilarious loops,
Telling tales of silly groups,
While we knit our hopes with a sneeze,
And unravel myths with perfect ease.

Colors clash in a riotous dance,
As sock puppets pull off their chance,
To thread the needle of cosmic hair,
And stitch together truths laid bare.

So grasp a thread, let laughter lead,
In this tapestry, plant the seed,
For every stitch and wacky twist,
Is a joyous truth we can't resist!

Guiding Lights in the Dark

When lost in a forest so deep,
I called out to squirrels for a peep.
They chuckled and pointed their tails,
Said, "Follow the moon, it never fails!"

In shadows where mischief does creep,
A firefly buzzed, 'Don't fear, just leap!'
I tripped on a root, what a sight,
And danced like a fool under night light!

Meditations on Boundless Passage

Two fish in a bowl played checkers all day,
Debating which ocean is better to sway.
One swam in circles, the other just frowned,
"Hurry up, mate, we're lost but not drowned!"

The clock on the wall was a turtle named Ted,
Who pondered on paths while spinning his head.
"Time's just a joke," he said with a grin,
"Let's roll to the future, that's where fun begins!"

The Unseen Cartographer's Love

My heart is a map drawn in crayon so bright,
With love scribbled in corners, what a sight!
But X marks the spot where I lost my way,
Chasing breadcrumbs, I thought they were stray.

An atlas once told me to always keep smiling,
But I tripped on a line and ended up styling.
With compass in hand and a sock on my foot,
My quest for romance has gone quite askew!

Tides of Wisdom Through the Ages

On a beach made of jellybeans, I sat,
With crabs in top hats discussing the chat.
"Use waves for your wisdom," said one with a grin,
"Just ride the foam, it's the wave of a win!"

As tides rolled in with a splash and a cheer,
I learned salty secrets from seaweed, oh dear!
"Don't take life too seriously, laugh and explore,
For wisdom tastes best when served with some s'more!"

Labyrinth of the Infinite Journey

In circles we spin, a dance with no end,
Lost in the giggles, a truth we pretend.
Maps drawn in crayons, our feet feel the beat,
Around and around, oh, this journey's a treat!

Paths made of jellybeans lead us astray,
Every turn's a chuckle, come join in the fray.
We chase after shadows, with signs upside down,
In a maze of our making, we wear the clown crown.

Each twist brings a riddle, a jester's delight,
With each clever answer, we burst into flight.
So here's to the wanderers, never in gloom,
In this laughter-filled labyrinth, we always find room!

So roll on, my friends, through this wacky expanse,
Where wisdom looks silly and laughs lead the dance.
In moments of joy, we capture the truth,
In the jest and the jangle, we reclaim our youth.

Portals to Unseen Realities

Through flaps of the curtains, a world shifts and shakes,
Bright hats on our heads, oh, the folly it makes!
We peek through the keyhole, then trip on our toes,
In dimensions of giggles, where anything goes.

The clocks play tick-tock, but they're off on their game,
Time folds like a napkin, or is it a frame?
With portals of sunshine, we swim through the air,
In realms of odd wonders, we dance without care.

Silly socks on our hands, who says that's unwise?
We leap through the laughter, with glimmering eyes.
Each door is a doorway to giggles galore,
In these vibrant dimensions, we're always wanting more.

So let's juggle our dreams and hop through the light,
In the portals of play, everything feels right.
Here's to the unseen, laughing hard as we play,
In the realm of absurdity, we'll forever stay!

The Unfolding of Ancient Wisdom

Old scrolls whisper secrets of what once was grand,
Yet here in the present, we're just trying to stand.
With wisdom that giggles, it surely is sly,
Unfolding like laundry hung out to dry.

We feast on the lessons, with socks that don't match,
In the garden of sarcasm, truths scratch and catch.
The wise old owl hoots, but we just hear the laugh,
In the chorus of nonsense, we find our own path.

So let's sit in a circle, with pies made of fluff,
Exchanging our stories, though they may get tough.
In wisdom's old bakery, we bake special treats,
Of laughter and nonsense, our friendship repeats.

So raise up your glasses, to silliness bright,
In the unfolding of wisdom, we'll shine through the night.

Amidst all the seriousness, find joy in the jest,
For in laughter we flourish, and surely feel blessed!

Oracles of the Eternal Now

Oh wise old oracle, what's the truth of today?
"Just order your pizza and let life decay!"
In the present, we stumble, yet giggle with glee,
The future is silly, it's as clear as can be.

With clocks made of rubber, they stretch and they bend,
Each tick is a giggle, a noodle, a friend.
The now is a balloon, we float and we flop,
In the wisdom of laughter, we're free to just drop.

Mystics in monkey suits dance around with the stars,
They say, "Living in moments won't leave you with scars."
With soup made of marshmallows and time in a jar,
Greet the now with a chuckle, let's shine like a star!

So join in the joy, oh so light and so free,
In the oracles' giggles, find depth in the tea.
In this instant of whimsy, let's twirl through the glow,
For the truth is a tickle, just laugh and let go!

Lanterns of Ancient Knowledge

In a cave filled with socks, they went to explore,
They found a sage snoring, and what a bore!
He woke up with wisdom, but spilt his tea,
Now ancient truths drip all over me.

A chicken crossed the road, to find some light,
But the lanterns were out, oh what a fright!
The sage scratched his head, "What's so profound?"
While socks danced around, making quite a sound.

Truths wrapped in riddles, like gifts gone astray,
The chicken just clucked, "I'm on my way!"
A journey begins, with giggles in tow,
In a world where advice comes with a crow.

So let's light up the night, with socks and with cheer,
As ancient knowledge shines bright, we all persevere.
With laughter as lanterns, we wander and roam,
Finding wisdom in socks, we finally feel home.

Reflections in the Still Waters

By the lake with some ducks, all floating around,
I spied a wise frog, his name was profound.
He croaked out confessions, of flies he once chased,
But his reflection was blurred; it looked quite misplaced.

The ducks quacked with laughter, they rolled in delight,
"Your wisdom's like dinner, it doesn't seem right!"
The frog puffed his chest, and cleared up the breeze,
"Look deeper, dear ducks, or just laugh as you please!"

A turtle swam past, with a shell full of tales,
A sea of confusion, with stories in gales.
"All truths must be told," he said with a grin,
Yet we just floated on, filled with giggles within.

At sunset we gathered, shadows began to dance,
The laughter echoed loudly—a whimsical chance.
In the still waters' mirror, the truth still eludes,
While silly old frogs share their dodgy old moods.

Chasing the Horizon of Truth

An ambitious young squirrel had dreams in his head,
"To solve all the mysteries!" he gleefully said.
He chased after shadows, and barked at the sun,
With nuts as his trophies, his quest was such fun!

The horizon kept teasing, just out of his reach,
He thought of wise lessons, oh how they could teach.
But each nut he collected turned to laughter with ease,
As the horizon just chuckled, "Come closer, if you please!"

A rabbit hopped by, with a watch on his wrist,
"Are you losing your time?" he smirked with a twist.
The squirrel just waved, "I'm chasing the light!"
While the rabbit just danced, under stars so bright.

With giggles as fuel, they wandered and played,
Filling their hearts with the joys that they made.
In chasing horizons, they found that delight
Can turn every search into a humorous flight.

Eternal Echoes of Reality

In a forest of whispers, a ghost tried to speak,
He mixed up his tales, and fright turned to squeak.
His stories were tangled, a hilarious fright,
As he drifted through shadows, while missing the light.

A raccoon chimed in, with a mask on his face,
"Your echoes are funny; that's a real saving grace!"
The ghost scratched his head, "Why can't I be clear?"
While raccoons rolled laughter, "Just drink some root beer!"

Each tale spun around like a whirlwind of glee,
The ghost took a sip, "Now I just want to be!"
A truth made of giggles wrapped in each sigh,
As echoes of humor floated up to the sky.

So here in the forest, reality bends,
With laughter like lyrics, that never quite ends.
The ghost and the raccoon, a whimsical pair,
In echoes of joy, they danced without care.

Veils of Reality Lifted

In a world where logic bends,
The foolish make amends,
Banana peels on polished floors,
Truth giggles, then it soars.

Umbrellas that promise to fly,
Get caught in a pie in the sky,
Yet wisdom wears mismatched socks,
Laughing as reason locks.

The jester dances on reason's stage,
While scholars lecture from a cage,
Silly hats upon serious heads,
Finding humor in sacred threads.

As veils part with a chuckle and cheer,
What's real is often quite unclear,
The truth can be quite a prank,
And laughter fills up the dank.

The Odyssey of the Unwritten

A journey begun on a diet of dreams,
Where nothing is as funny as it seems,
We write tales with crayons so bright,
Making knights of salad, what a sight!

Wandering through fields of lost ideas,
Where laughter conceals our greatest fears,
A tiger in slippers, oh what a view,
He debates with a cat named Lou.

We sail on ships of never-ending ink,
Rescuing stories that never could stink,
With mermaids serving us fizzy drinks,
As we ponder on the what-ifs and winks.

Each page a world that makes us chime,
In the odyssey of non-sensical rhyme,
Life scribbles down absurd sayings,
Here's to joy in wild playings!

Sails of the Navigating Spirit

With sails made from cotton candy clouds,
We drift through the land where laughter crowds,
Navigating with a wink and a nod,
As wisdom moonwalks like a cosmic clod.

Lost in a sea of mismatched socks,
Where all roads lead to jammy docks,
Sailing with fish that tell bad jokes,
Who argue if cats are men in cloaks.

Our vessel's name is Happy Mistake,
Charting where giggles surface and quake,
Every wave whispers secrets of glee,
With the crew composed of bright bumblebees.

So let the winds of absurdity blow,
As we drift with a side of woe,
For in nonsense, we find our best art,
Sailing on whims that tickle the heart.

Illumination on the Path of Shadows

In shadows where giggles softly blend,
We chase after truths that refuse to end,
With flashlights made of marshmallow fluff,
Illuminating paths that are just too tough.

Each corner holds a sock puppet sage,
Who tells us the past is just a stage,
Where clowns parade with stories of old,
And truth wears a wig made of gold.

Jokes flicker like fireflies in flight,
As we wander in the echoes of the night,
The moon snickers, a sly little glow,
While shadows shuffle, putting on a show.

So dance beneath the twinkling lore,
Where truths are absurd—forever more,
In the path of laughter, we gently glide,
Finding joy in shadows, side by side.

Luminaries of the Ageless Quest

In a quest for wisdom, I lost my way,
Chased a shadow that danced in the day.
My map, it crinkled, my compass went mad,
Turned right at a squirrel, now isn't that bad?

Time rolled ahead, thought I'd take a break,
Found a wise turtle having lunch by a lake.
He said, "Kid, slow down, you're missing the fun,"
So now I'm just laughing, till the quest is done.

I followed a rabbit with a hat and a grin,
He chuckled and said, "Where to begin?"
With wisdom that sparkled and mischief galore,
Time's just a joke that I can't ignore.

With stars overhead, I danced through the night,
Trip on my dreams, oh what a sight!
If age is a number, I'll lose track of mine,
For joy is eternal and oh, so divine!

Beyond the Constraints of Time

I bought a clock that ticks backward, you see,
It's perfect for days when I just want to flee.
Set my hours to giggles, my minutes to glee,
I'm late for my life, but just on a spree!

Time travel's tricky, or so I was told,
But I found a wormhole that's awfully bold.
It took me to lunch with a dinosaur, wow!
We dined on some pizza and cheese from a cow.

Zipping through ages with laughter and cheer,
Met Cleopatra, she said, "Bring me a beer!"
But my mug was all empty, a time-travel flop,
We ended up sipping on water—bikini top!

So here's to the fun, the mishaps, the jest,
Time's really just foam on a quirk-laden quest.
With giggles as anchors, I'm starting to see,
Timeless adventures, forever carefree!

Notes from the Timeless Traveler

I found a postcard from the future today,
Says, "Don't worry, you'll find a buffet."
With pizza on Mars and ice cream on the sun,
The timeless traveler's life is so much fun!

I packed my bags full of laughter and jokes,
Hitched a ride on a comet with cartoonish folks.
We crashed a tea party with robots and cats,
And danced with the fairies wearing funky hats!

"Time is a river," the wise old owl said,
I wore my rubber ducky, he wore a red fed.
We chased after moments, oh what a delight,
With giggles and zingers till the morning light.

So if you see me in times yet to come,
Know I'm still laughing—oh isn't that fun?
Just jotting my notes on the whims of the past,
Traveling through ages, making moments that last!

Navigating Heartbeats of History

In a boat made of giggles, I sailed through the years,
With laughter as my compass, and joy as my gears.
I met a king who was ticklish, oh what a scene,
He giggled with glee, 'till he turned bright green!

Time's like a dancehall, spinning us round,
With disco balls shining, oh what a sound.
My shoes made of candy, I twirled to the beat,
While history chuckled at my colourful feet.

A knight on a llama joined in on our spree,
He yelled, "Fear not, friends! I bring victory!"
But tripped on his sword, and fell for a laugh,
As giggles erupted from the townsfolk's half.

So here's to heartbeats that skip with delight,
With laughter as armor, we're ready to fight!
In the realm of all ages, I'll dance any day,
For humor's the key that lights up the way!

Anchors to the Ageless Soul

In a world where seconds fly,
I chase time like a pie in the sky.
With clocks that giggle, laugh and tease,
I ponder life while swinging from trees.

I've found wisdom in a rubber chicken,
A timeless beacon, always kickin'.
With each hoot of my grandpa's old chair,
I anchor thoughts in the breeze of the air.

A sticky note says, "Don't take the bait!"
Yet here I sit, sipping on fate.
Who needs a map when you've got a grin?
In the circus of life, let the fun begin!

So laugh with me, let your worries fade,
As we dance around this merry glade.
With age as a friend, let's take a stroll,
For laughter is an anchor for the soul.

Whispers from the Forgotten Past

I found a diary from days gone by,
Filled with doodles of a cat in the sky.
It spoke of lunch with a talking shoe,
And dates with shadows that giggled, it's true!

Mysteries unfold like a soggy pizza,
Each slice a memory, artful and cheetah.
A time-machine made of duct tape and dreams,
Takes me back where nothing's as it seems.

Oh! The time that I mistook a sock for my shoe,
Got lost in the laughter, that laugh made me blue.
With ghosts that moonwalk and angels that sing,
The past is a playground where whimsy is king!

So come take a trip down this wacky lane,
Where sandwiches dance in the midst of the rain.
With tales to cherish, let's giggle and trust,
In whispers where laughter's a must!

Mapmakers of the Mind

In my head, a jigsaw's skewed and jumbled,
Pieces of wisdom that often stumble.
With crayons I chart this wild terrain,
Each color a thought, a knot in the brain.

There's X marks the spot where I lost my keys,
And arrows point out where I sneeze with ease.
A wasp with a monocle leads me astray,
But giggles emerge as I wander and play.

I draw roads of cheese and marshmallow hills,
In this quirky land, creativity thrills.
I travel through clouds made of cotton candy,
Sipping on lemonade, oh isn't that dandy?

So let's map out our dreams in this jolly way,
With giggling skunks and a sun made of hay.
Together let's wander, with laughter in mind,
In this fanciful world where we leave dull behind!

Celestial Navigation of the Spirit

I boldly sail through a galaxy hot,
Navigating stardust, oh what a plot!
With tin foil wings and a hat made of cheese,
I dance with the comets, as light as a breeze.

My compass is broken, it points to my fridge,
Where snacks whisper secrets, oh what a smidge!
I cartwheel through planets with a bounce in my step,
As aliens giggle, "Hey, dude, that's hep!"

With each passing star, I chuckle and sway,
In this vast universe, I've lost my way.
But laughter's my anchor, my guiding North Star,
Bringing joy to the journey, no matter how far.

So join me, dear friend, on this flight through the light,
Where meaning is floating like bubbles in flight.
With the universe chuckling, oh so sincere,
Life's an adventure, let's hold it so dear!

Eternal Navigators

In a boat made of dreams, we sail with glee,
Tangled maps and cup of tea.
The stars all wink, say 'trust your heart',
We giggle aloud, it's a silly art.

With pencils for compasses, we draw the skies,
Navigating laughter, with joyful lies.
Each wave a chuckle, each breeze a joke,
We steer through clouds like a silly bloke.

Our sails are full of wishes and hopes,
Riding on whimsy, we do the ropes.
Whichever way the wind might blow,
We follow the giggles, where they go!

So raise your glasses and toast the fate,
To merry sailors, and a life first-rate!
We wander the sea with hearts so bold,
Laughing at treasures that time has told.

Anchors of Clarity

Who needs a guide when you've got your shoes?
Just follow your nose, ignore the blues.
Anchored in nonsense, we find our way,
Each mistake a dance, we shout hooray!

We dropped our anchors in a big ice cream,
Thought we found wisdom, but it was a dream.
Each scoop of joy, a lesson we find,
Wobbling around, rocking unconfined.

With every splash, a laugh erupts loud,
We're anchored together, a silly crowd.
The tides of truth pull us side to side,
Clarity's fog, our beloved guide.

So let's sail on with sprinkles and cheer,
In the hull of nonsense, there's nothing to fear!
With banter and jokes, we brave the storm,
For laughter's the anchor that keeps us warm.

The Scrolls of Existence

With a parchment of giggles, we write our fate,
Scrolls of existence, oh isn't it great?
Every twist and turn, it's a comedy show,
Life's punchlines land, just as they flow!

We pen down our whims on a wobbly board,
Silly script dances, like a playful sword.
Jokes in the margins, wisdom in rhyme,
A scroll full of chuckles, it's all quite fine!

With ink made of laughter, we draw out the light,
The scrolls of existence, what a delight!
Funny little doodles, a jester's parade,
In the book of our lives, joy does not fade.

So let's open the scrolls and read 'em aloud,
Embrace the absurd, we fit like a cloud!
Each tale is a giggle, each truth a jest,
Life's scrolls of existence, we're truly blessed.

Footprints of the Universe

Step by step in cosmic shoes,
Dancing through stardust, we can't lose.
Each footprint left is a laugh, you see,
Tracing silly patterns, wild and free.

The universe chuckles as we skip,
Making goofy shapes, a cosmic trip.
Every step a whimsy, a spark of fun,
Creating our path under the sun.

We twirl through galaxies, leave marks behind,
Silly imprints that don't seem to mind.
In the fabric of space, we laugh and play,
Footprints of joy, going our way.

So join us, dear friends, in this cosmic race,
With giggles and grins, there's joy to embrace!
Follow the footprints, wherever they lead,
In the universe's jest, we find what we need.

Seeker's Guide to the Infinite

A guide was lost in life's big mall,
Took a right, but then hit a wall.
He asked a squirrel for some advice,
"Your compass is nuts! Just roll the dice!"

He bought a map marked with a smile,
It led him to wander for a mile.
Found an island of rubber ducks,
Turns out, they know all about luck!

A frog in a tux joined the quest,
"You're dressed to impress, but at best!"
They laughed and danced; what a surprise,
The truth was in twinkles, not in the skies!

In this journey of twists and turns,
The seeker learned that chuckles burn.
The infinite path was paved with cheer,
Who knew wisdom was found in a beer?

The Mirror of Endless Reflections

Stood before a mirror, look at me!
Reflections played like a funny CD.
My nose grew long; I turned to flee,
The image winked, called, "Have some tea!"

An echo laughed, a rhyme took flight,
"You look like my cousin who's quite a sight!"
We danced shadows on the tiled floor,
Gravity? Nah! Just humor to explore!

"Oh mirror, oh mirror, am I quite absurd?"
It replied, "Buddy, truth's a silly herd!"
Laugh lines grew; the secret was clear,
Being serious? Now that's a real fear!

In endless reflections, joy did abound,
The search for truth was silly, profound.
The mirror grinned, showing me glee,
It whispered, "Just laugh, and you'll be free!"

Footprints on Celestial Sands

On cosmic shores, I skipped and played,
Footprints drew lines like they were displayed.
Every step, a giggle, a hop, a prance,
As stars twinkled down, urging for a dance!

I tripped on a comet, fell into a laugh,
A stellar crab tried to draw a graph.
"We're all just grains on this sandy beach,"
"Now come have some fun, that's what I preach!"

A wink from a moonbeam told me to stay,
"Truth's found in laughter, not in cliché."
With laughter and quirks, we built a sand throne,
Each chuckle, a gem, each smile, a stone!

So dance on stardust, embrace the bizarre,
In celestial sands, we'll laugh near and far.
Leaving footprints, but memories last,
The wisdom we find? Oh, it's a blast!

Secrets of the Universe Unraveled

In a lab of "what ifs," I tested a thought,
Found out that gravity's kinda distraught.
A cat in a box scratched out the clue,
"The secret's in laughter, just look at the view!"

Galaxies giggled; they played hide and seek,
Black holes laughed deep, not at all meek.
Each star had a joke, a twisted punchline,
Echoing joy in the vast design!

I asked the sun, "What's life all about?"
He grinned, "It's warm, don't fear a doubt!"
Planets aligned, sharing snacks of delight,
While asteroids rolled in a cosmic fight!

So the universe winked as I sat in awe,
The truth laughed with me, revealing its flaw.
The secrets unraveled, so bright, so bold,
The funny is timeless; that's what I've told!

Threads of Destiny and Dreams

In a world made of yarn, I found a strange thread,
It tangled my thoughts and teased at my head.
A stitch in time saves nine, or so they say,
But this one made me dance in a wobbly way.

A needle in hand, I poked at my fate,
But all I could craft was a lopsided plate.
With magic and mayhem, I spun like a top,
Next thing I knew, I was housing a mop.

I wove in some laughter, a dash of delight,
But ended up lost in the fabric of night.
My threads of ambition pulled me far and wide,
Yet here I am, laughing, just along for the ride.

So here's to the dreams that keep us awake,
And threads that connect each strange move we make.
With a twist and a turn, let absurdity reign,
For destiny's fabric is frayed and it's plain.

Timeless Chimes in the Silence

Tick tock, said the clock, with a wink and a grin,
It chimed out a riddle, drew me right in.
In the hush of the night, I heard bongs of delight,
As the rooster took flight at the dreamer's twilight.

The bells chimed nonsense, a merry old tune,
Spinning tales of absurdity under the moon.
A ballet of tickles danced on my wall,
As silence erupted in a whimsical brawl.

A whimsical waltz, with no footwork to speak,
The ghosts serenaded me, both playful and bleak.
Each tick a reminder, of laughter and fun,
In the echo of chimes, where time's just begun.

So let's raise our mugs to the jests that unite,
In the silence of moments, a goblin delight.
With every odd chime, let's revel and sing,
For the party of time, oh, what joy it can bring!

The Needle of Introspection

With a needle of thought, I pricked my own brain,
Awakening wisdom, bringing joy and some pain.
Each poke was a question, each stab an idea,
But mostly it tickled, and oh, what a cheer!

I stitched up my feelings, quilted by hand,
But forgot where I put it, oh, isn't that grand?
Searching for answers in cupboards of fate,
I found a lost sock and an old dinner plate.

I sewed up my worries with bright colored threads,
But when I looked closer, they turned into beds.
I tumbled in laughter, a jester's wild ride,
For introspection is best when we slip, fall, and slide.

So poke, prod, and giggle, let chaos ensue,
For self-discovery's a show full of flue.
In the merry mayhem, let's stitch with a cheer,
For wisdom is best when it's wrapped up in sneers.

Charting the Course of Awareness

Here in a boat made of thoughts and confetti,
I sailed on the sea, but my sails weren't ready.
The map was a doodle, the compass a joke,
Each wave whispered wisdom, but mostly it spoke.

I navigated circles, a dizzying dance,
With pirates of laughter that led me by chance.
They shouted their secrets, while raiding my snacks,
And I laughed so hard, I just fell through the cracks.

Awareness is tricky, a playful old sprite,
It hides in the corners when the mood feels just right.
With a splash and a giggle, I charted it sly,
As the gulls serenaded me, singing "Oh my!"

So let's row through the nonsense, with joy on our breeze,

For the course of awareness is best with some cheese.
In the boat of oblivion, we'll sail side by side,
Chasing laughter and whimsy, on this whimsical ride.

Navigating Eternal Paths

Oh, how we wander with laughs and glee,
Following paths of whimsy, you see!
A map that scribbles, all zigzag and spry,
Makes every lost turn feel like flying high.

With a compass that points to where it feels best,
We navigate life like a silly jest.
Lost socks and odd keys lead the way,
Let's dance in circles, come what may!

Round and round on this path we spin,
Chasing the sunset with a wide, goofy grin.
Every misstep becomes a delight,
As we laugh with each twist in our flight.

So here's to the folly of timeless strolls,
With absurd detours becoming our goals.
Even the maps don't know where to go,
But who cares? We'll just put on a show!

Whispers of the Ancients

Listen closely to tales of yore,
Ancient folks had jokes galore!
They mapped the stars, but missed the sun,
Life's big riddle, all in good fun.

With rocks and sticks as their guide,
They ventured forth, full of pride!
But oops, they tripped over a tree,
Yet laughed it off, as you can see.

Wisdom comically carved in stone,
Echoes back: 'You're never alone!'
So dance like a dodo, twirl like a whiz,
In the ancient games, we find our fizz.

Join the laughter, embrace the jest,
For truth goes where the giggles rest.
With each silly whisper hanging in air,
We learn that laughter is always fair!

Timeless Signposts

Pointing this way, or maybe that,
The signposts argue like a chatty cat!
One says 'left,' the other says 'right,'
But who needs a guide when it feels so bright?

With arrows that dance and twirl around,
In this big circus, we're all spellbound.
We'll ignore the signs that don't make sense,
And find our way with laughable hints.

So let's follow whims and dashes of fun,
Wherever we go, we'll never be done!
Each trip a jolly, tangled affair,
And laughter's direction will get us everywhere!

So raise your flag and make a toast,
To the great adventure we love the most!
With timeless signposts that can be silly,
We'll keep on smiling, oh what a willy!

The Map of Infinite Horizons

A map rolled out with crayon delight,
Shows infinite places all in plain sight.
But wait! There's a scribble on this part,
Let's chase it down, it's where we start!

With an 'X' that marks a place that's wild,
An adventure awaits for every child.
Navigating through giggles and stuff,
We'll take each turn, we can't get enough!

The horizon laughs as we race to the end,
With a jolly ol' map, oh what a friend!
Past each edge, where time seems to bend,
We'll find where the real fun trends!

So let's unfold dreams, with colors so brave,
In the land of the silly, we'll always save.
Maps may lead us to places anew,
But fun is the treasure, it's all true!

Echoes of the Unseen

In a world that spins with glee,
We search for truths, like lost TV.
The clocks tick on, but do they know?
We wear our socks, mismatched in tow.

When the sun winks at the toaster,
It asks, "Why don't we need a coaster?"
The shadows dance, they trip and tumble,
Laughing at our serious fumble.

Invisible threads pull us near,
Yet all I see is my missing beer.
As wisdom slips between my buys,
Socks vanish, and I hear the flies.

So let's chase dreams with silly hats,
Waddle like ducks and chat with cats.
In this playground of the unseen ride,
We're all just clowns, let's enjoy the slide.

Guiding Stars in Infinite Skies

Stars dangle like candy on a string,
Wishing on them makes the heart sing.
Yet here I am, confused by my map,
With pickle jars in my neighborhood gap.

Navigating life like a kite on a breeze,
Dodging raindrops while wobbly on knees.
The moon's advice is quite absurd,
'Take it easy, like a sleeping bird.'

Asteroids float like old socks at night,
Wondering why we don't just take flight.
With donuts shaped like distant stars,
I'll navigate with snacks, not cars.

So here's my wish upon this pie,
That laughter will take me up high.
Let's count the laughs, disregard the fears,
As we dance our way through the years.

Threads of Memory and Fate

Memories are like tangled hair,
Easily lost but hard to declare.
I'll knit them together with laughter and time,
While sipping my tea from a shoe that's sublime.

Each thread tells a story, some wild, some sweet,
Of ice cream fights and running on feet.
With a garden of gnomes who won't take a break,
We'll weave silly truths for the humor's sake.

Fate throws dice behind the closed door,
Laughing at choices we made before.
Knitting yarn with secrets in tow,
The cat sneaks in and steals the show.

So let's unravel this wondrous game,
Share our tales, while forgetting blame.
For each silly moment a fabric we weave,
In this fashion of fun, we all will believe.

Secrets Carved in Time

Carved in the bark of an ancient tree,
Are secrets that tickle, just like a bee.
They giggle and wiggle, then disappear,
Just like my diet, oh dear, oh dear!

In the sands of time, footprints do dance,
Whispering tales of an awkward romance.
The sun laughs loudly, and the moon gives a grin,
While I trip over words, akin to a spin.

Calendar pages fly off with a cheer,
I stop and pause for my pickle jar's beer.
With each passing tick, I shrug with delight,
Wishing for cats in a world full of light.

So let's toast to the moments that make us feel bold,
To secrets that bubble and stories untold.
In the dance of today, let's giggle and roam,
For laughter and joy, they'll always feel home.